Masters of Music
THE WORLD'S GREATEST COMPOSERS

The Life and Times of

Felix Mendelssohn

Mitchell Lane
PUBLISHERS

P.O. Box 196
Hockessin, Delaware 19707

Masters of Music
THE WORLD'S GREATEST COMPOSERS

Titles in the Series
The Life and Times of...

Johann Sebastian Bach

Ludwig van Beethoven

Irving Berlin

Hector Berlioz

Leonard Bernstein

Johannes Brahms

Frederic Chopin

Duke Ellington

Stephen Foster

George Gershwin

William Gilbert and Arthur Sullivan

George Frideric Handel

Franz Joseph Haydn

Scott Joplin

Franz Liszt

Felix Mendelssohn

Wolfgang Amadeus Mozart

Franz Peter Schubert

John Philip Sousa

Igor Stravinsky

Peter Ilyich Tchaikovsky

Giuseppe Verdi

Antonio Lucio Vivaldi

Richard Wagner

Visit us on the web: www.mitchelllane.com
Comments? email us: mitchelllane@mitchelllane.com

Masters of Music
THE WORLD'S GREATEST COMPOSERS

The Life and Times of

Felix Mendelssohn

by Susan Zannos

Mitchell Lane
PUBLISHERS

Printing   2   3   4   5   6   7   8

Library of Congress Cataloging-in-Publication Data
Zannos, Susan.
    The life and times of Felix Mendelssohn/Susan Zannos.
        p. cm. — (Masters of music. The world's greatest composers)
    Summary: A biography of the nineteenth-century German composer.
    Includes bibliographical references (p.) and index.
     ISBN 1-58415-210-9 (lib bdg.)
    1. Mendelssohn-Bartholdy, Felix, 1809-1847—Juvenile literature. 2. Composers—Germany—Biography—Juvenile literature. [1. Mendelssohn-Bartholdy, Felix, 1809-1847. 2. Composers.] I. Title. II. Series.
ML3930.M44Z26
780'.92—dc21   2003000348

JB MENDELSSOHN, F. c.1

ABOUT THE AUTHOR: Susan Zannos has been a lifelong educator, having taught at all levels, from preschool to college, in Mexico, Greece, Italy, Russia, and Lithuania, as well as in the United States. She has published a mystery *Trust the Liar* (Walker and Co.) and *Human Types: Essence and the Enneagram* (Samuel Weiser). Her book, *Human Types*, was recently translated into Russian, and in 2003 Susan was invited to tour Russia and lecture about her book. Another book she wrote for young adults, *Careers in Education* (Mitchell Lane) was selected for the New York Public Library's "Books for the Teen Age 2003 List." She has written many books for children, including *Chester Carlson and the Development of Xerography* and *The Life and Times of Ludwig van Beethoven* (Mitchell Lane). Her great interest in composers inspired her to write this book. When not traveling, Susan lives in the Sierra Foothills of Northern California.

PHOTO CREDITS: Cover: Archivo Iconografico, SA/Corbis; p. 6 Corbis; p. 11 Barnabas Bosshart/Corbis; p. 13 Photo Researchers; p. 14 Hulton/Archive; p. 17 Reuters/Corbis; p. 18 Getty Images; p. 21 AP Photo; p. 22 Hulton/Archive; pp.26, 27 Bettmann/Corbis; p. 29 Corbis; p. 30 Corbis; p. 35 Corbis; p. 36 Bettmann/Corbis; p. 43 Gianni Dagli Orti/Corbis.

PUBLISHER'S NOTE: This story is based on the author's extensive research, which she believes to be accurate. Documentation of such research is contained on page 46.

The internet sites referenced herein were active as of the publication date. Due to the fleeting nature of some Web sites, we cannot guarantee they will all be active when you are reading this book.

Contents

The Life and Times of
Felix Mendelssohn

by Susan Zannos

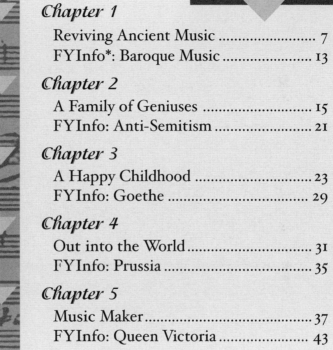

Chapter 1
Reviving Ancient Music 7
FYInfo*: Baroque Music 13

Chapter 2
A Family of Geniuses 15
FYInfo: Anti-Semitism 21

Chapter 3
A Happy Childhood 23
FYInfo: Goethe 29

Chapter 4
Out into the World.............................. 31
FYInfo: Prussia 35

Chapter 5
Music Maker....................................... 37
FYInfo: Queen Victoria 43

Selected Works 44
Chronology... 44
Timeline in History 45
Further Reading 46
Works Consulted 46
Glossary 47
Index 48
* For Your Information

Johann Sebastian Bach was the greatest of the German baroque composers. Some people believe he was the greatest composer of all time. After Bach's death in 1750, his music was seldom played. Many musicians thought Bach's compositions were old fashioned. The vocal music, such as the magnificent St. Matthew Passion, was difficult to perform and required a highly trained choir. In spite of the difficulties, young Felix Mendelssohn directed a successful revival of Bach's vocal masterpiece in 1829.

Reviving Ancient Music

In 1823 when Felix Mendelssohn was fourteen years old, his grandmother gave him a very special Christmas present. It was a copy of Johann Sebastian Bach's oratorio *St. Matthew Passion*.

Why was Felix so happy with that gift? An ordinary German boy at that time would have had no interest in the works of Johann Sebastian Bach, who had died more than 70 years earlier. His music was considered to be as outdated as the dreamy pop ballads of the 1930s are to today's young people.

But Felix was no ordinary boy. He was a musical genius comparable to the young Wolfgang Amadeus Mozart. He played the piano publicly when he was nine. By the time Felix was fourteen, he had written music of excellent quality, as Mozart had by the same age.

Some of Bach's instrumental music was still familiar to serious musicians. Felix's most important music teacher, Carl Zelter, had studied with a man who had been a student of Bach. Felix himself had learned to play many of Bach's preludes and fugues.

But Bach's great choral masterpieces were considered old-fashioned and had been virtually forgotten. The *St. Matthew Passion* had not been performed since Bach's death in 1750. Not surprisingly, it wasn't easy to find copies.

Zelter had one. Apparently he let Felix, his favorite student, have a few peeks. That was all the youngster needed. In his imagination, he could hear the glorious voices. So he desperately wanted a copy of his own.

Babette Salomon, Felix's grandmother, lived in Paris. She had a good friend who collected old music manuscripts. One was the *St. Matthew Passion*. She asked him for it, and gave it to Felix.

Because the copy was nearly 100 years old, it had faded badly and was hard to read. That didn't matter to Felix. He went over it again and again. He made notes in the margins. He carefully copied out sections. His sisters helped him by copying the vocal parts and practicing them. And he did all this without ever believing that the work could be performed.

During the next few years, Felix began asking some of his other friends to sing some of the parts. One of them, Therese Devrient, described an evening at the Mendelssohns' house. "Felix would sit at the piano, pale and excited," she wrote. "We the singers stood around him so that he could at all times see us. That was very necessary. Not only did we experience difficulty in singing the music by sight, but both the notes and the text were so illegible that it was almost impossible to make sense of them. Yet we were terribly moved and felt that we had been transported into a new world of music."

Therese's brother Eduard Devrient was so excited by the power of the music that he told Felix they had to perform the

entire *St. Matthew Passion* in public. Felix would conduct, while Eduard would sing the central role of Jesus. Felix realized that Eduard was right. But they would need many more singers than the small groups that gathered around the Mendelssohns' piano.

So the two young men approached Zelter. He was the director of the Berlin Singakademie, the city's most prestigious musical organization.

But even though he was Felix's teacher and both Felix and Eduard had sung with the Singakademie, he gave many reasons why the performance was impossible. The *Passion* needed the kind of choirs Bach had trained himself. The music was too difficult. A performance would need a double orchestra of the highest ability. They would need many long and difficult rehearsals. The list of objections went on and on.

The objections didn't deter Felix and Eduard. They told the director that they were sure they could do it. They had already worked on the score for a long time. They praised Zelter for his work in developing the fine choir of the Singakadamie. And, they added, he should encourage his students to try something daring on their own.

Finally Zelter gave in. The young men immediately began their preparations. It was to be a charity event to help a sewing school for poor girls. The Mendelssohn family paid for the rental of the hall. Felix didn't charge anything for his work as conductor.

In addition to the soloists, they had 400 singers in two cho-ruses. There were also dozens of orchestra members. Everyone got together for nine full rehearsals of the score that Felix had worked on for years.

"All were amazed," Devrient wrote, "at its dramatic power. No one had ever suspected old Bach of all this."

The growing excitement of the musicians was contagious. When news got out about the performance, all 400 tickets were sold almost immediately. A thousand more people gathered outside the theater on March 11, 1829, the night of the performance.

It was a sensation.

The most important members of the cultural community of Berlin were there. Many in the audience wept with emotion. It was such a great success they repeated the performance ten days later on Bach's birthday.

"This marked the first time in history that a major work by a composer who had fallen markedly out of favor had been reconsidered and hailed as an important masterwork," wrote Stephen Ledbetter of the Academy of Ancient Music. "The excitement that surrounded the performance led quickly to further revivals of Bach."

Several things about Felix Mendelssohn are evident from this event early in his musical career.

For one thing, he came from a wealthy family. Many composers had to struggle to make a living. Mozart lived and died in poverty. Ludwig van Beethoven resented the demands of his wealthy patrons. Joseph Haydn's employer treated him like a servant. But Mendelssohn never had to worry about money.

For another, Felix was no spoiled rich boy. He worked hard all his life. He was a perfectionist who insisted on rehearsing and rehearsing until the performance of the musicians was as good as it could possibly be.

This portrait bust of Felix Mendelssohn was placed outside his birthplace in Germany after the Second World War. In Nazi Germany all efforts were made to remove any memorials to artists of Jewish background. Statues of Mendelssohn were torn down and destroyed. His music was forbidden to be played. Only in the latter part of the Twentieth Century has this musical genius been acknowledged in his own country.

It also shows Felix's love of great music. He was not like other composers who were interested only in performing their own work. He wanted to perform the greatest music. He particularly wanted to perform music that had been neglected.

Still another quality that Felix Mendelssohn had was self-confidence and determination. He hardly ever doubted his own ability. He knew which music by other composers was truly great. He worked and revised his own music until it, too, was truly great. And once he was satisfied with the quality of his music, he trusted his skill in performing it.

And though it wasn't obvious, Felix's triumph actually began many years earlier when a young man with a serious deformity made a long walk.

He had been born almost exactly 100 years earlier. ◆

Baroque Music FYInfo

George Frideric Handel

"Baroque" comes from a French word that means "bizarre" or "fantastic." It was first used to describe the highly decorated churches and public buildings in Germany and Austria during the 17th and 18th Centuries. These buildings had fancy carvings of cherubs and angels, flowers and fruit, ribbons and bows, birds and animals—in fact, almost anything the sculptors could think of for decoration. Later the word was also used to describe the music of this period. During the high baroque period from 1700 to 1750, composers wrote music that was highly decorated, too.

Some of the great composers of the baroque period were the Italians Antonio Vivaldi, Arcangelo Corelli and Domenico Scarlatti, and the Germans George Frideric Handel and Johann Sebastian Bach. They knew each other personally, or at least were familiar with each other's music.

Baroque music is complex. It has contrasting elements with fancy ornaments. A lot of baroque music is church music, such as oratorios, that alternated solo voices with chorus and orchestra.

One technique used in baroque music is counterpoint. Contrapuntal music has contrasting melodies or musical themes. These are woven in and out and developed in contrast to each other according to strict laws of composition. The fugue was one form of counterpoint technique. A fugue uses one musical subject or theme and then expresses that subject in different ways.

A simple kind of fugue is a canon, which imitates the subject exactly but at different times. We all know canons like "Row, Row, Row Your Boat" or "Frere Jacques." One voice or group of voices starts. After the first phrase of the melody a second voice comes in, and then a third, and so on. Fugues can be much more complex than simple canons. The melody might play at different rhythms, one version with long notes and one with slow notes. The melody might even be played backwards!

Fortunately most of the baroque composers were also music teachers. They wrote examples for their students, like Johann Sebastian Bach's *Two Part Inventions*. These works helped not only their students but also musicians who came later to understand baroque music.

Felix Mendelssohn's birthplace, Hamburg, Germany, was an important port city. Abraham Mendelssohn, Felix's father, made a fortune in Hamburg by financing merchants who defied Napoleon's blockade and smuggled goods to England. When Felix was only two years old, the family was forced to flee from the military forces Napoleon sent to Hamburg.

CHAPTER

2

A Family of Geniuses

F elix was not the first genius in his family. His grandfather, Moses Mendelssohn, became a philosopher whose fame spread through all of Europe.

But no one could have predicted Moses' sparkling future after his birth in Dessau in 1729. The boy had three things going against him. Because of a childhood illness, he was a hunchback. He stammered. And he was Jewish.

Moses knew that without education he would have a life as a poor peddler since no other jobs were open to Jews. His teacher, David Frankel, moved to Berlin to be chief rabbi in 1743. So the 14-year-old Moses begged his parents to let him follow Frankel.

He walked the entire distance of about 80 miles. There was only one entrance to the city through which a Jew could pass. The guard at the gate asked Moses why he wanted to enter Berlin. The boy replied with the one German word he knew: "*lernen*." To learn. On that day the guard recorded, "Today there passed through Rosenthaler Gate, six oxen, seven pigs, one Jew."

Moses found his teacher in the crowded ghetto where all Jews had to live. He faithfully attended lectures on Jewish law, but he

also eagerly studied many other subjects. He quickly learned German. One of the first German books he read was about the Protestant religion. It was his first awareness of religions other than his own. He read literature, philosophy, and science. He studied more languages, and taught himself Latin.

Soon he became known throughout the Jewish community of Berlin for his scholarship. A wealthy Jewish merchant hired him to tutor his four children, so Moses moved out of his cold attic room into a room in a comfortable house. Later, after the children had grown and no longer needed a tutor, the merchant gave Moses Mendelssohn a job as a bookkeeper in his factory. Eventually he became a full partner and a wealthy man.

He kept studying. And he had begun to write.

His writing attracted other young philosophers and artists, many of them outside the Jewish community. Eventually his books were translated into many other languages.

When he was 33 years old, Moses visited Hamburg and met Fromet Guggenheim. She knew and admired his writing, but when she saw him she was shocked at his ugly appearance. When she began crying, Moses told her a story. When a Jewish child is born, he explained, the name of the person he or she will marry is announced in heaven. When he—Moses—was born, he said, his future wife was named. It was said that she would be a humpback. So Moses said, "A deformed girl will be bitter and unhappy. Dear Lord, let me have the humpback and make the girl flawless and beautiful."

Fromet was so charmed by the story that she agreed to marry Moses. Six children, three sons and three daughters, survived to

adulthood. Moses not only taught his children himself but also hired the best tutors to educate them.

Abraham Mendelssohn, Felix's father, was Moses Mendelssohn's second son. When Felix became famous, Abraham said, "Formerly I was known as the son of my father; now I am known as the father of my son."

While Abraham did not achieve the fame of either his father or his son, he had a kind of genius of his own: he made lots of money as a banker. He married Lea Salomon, an educated and talented woman he met in Paris. They moved to Hamburg where Abraham went into a banking partnership with his brother Joseph.

Hamburg was a port city dependent upon the shipping trade. When Napoleon attempted to blockade England, many Hamburg

This simple gravestone marks the final resting place of Moses Mendelssohn, one of the most famous and respected philosophers of the 18th Century. Although crippled with a humpback and unable to speak without stammering, this brilliant man became successful both intellectually and in business. Moses was the grandfather of composer Felix Mendelssohn.

merchants decided to ignore Napoleon's orders and smuggle their goods to England. They became wealthy running the blockade, and so did their bankers. While Abraham and Lea were becoming rich, they were also starting their family. Their first child, Fanny, was born in 1805. Next came Felix on February 3, 1809, then Rebecka in 1811.

But only a few weeks after Rebecka was born, the family had to run for their lives as Napoleon sent his military forces to Hamburg. With their three small children and one very large fortune, they fled to Berlin. Their fourth child, Paul, was born there in 1813.

Napoleon Bonaparte was the military leader who led the French army to victory after victory in the years following the French Revolution. The other countries of Europe attacked France, but for several years Napoleon defeated them all. His blockade of England enabled the Mendelssohn family to become wealthy by smuggling goods.

As his father had before him, Abraham Mendelssohn gave his children the best education he could afford. Since he was very wealthy he could afford the very best tutors.

All four children, but especially the older two, were talented in music. Felix very early showed signs of musical genius. And there may have been another genius in the family. Many of their friends considered Fanny to be a more brilliant pianist than her brother. Eduard Devrient remembered that Felix's playing was "extraordinarily dextrous and possessed of great musical assurance," but "did not equal that of his older sister Fanny." Another family friend found that Fanny was Felix's "equal in composition and piano-forte playing."

The two children were very close. They admired and respected each other. When he was thirteen years old and she was seventeen, she wrote, "I have always been his only musical adviser, and he never writes down a thought without submitting it to my judgment. For instance, I have known his operas by heart before a note was written."

Yet it must have been painful for Fanny to see Felix have all the opportunities that she would have liked to have. Her parents did not support Fanny's desire for a musical career. Her father told her that it would not be suitable for a woman to be a professional musician.

Perhaps Fanny did not easily give up her music. She had not yet married by the time she was twenty-three. At that point, her father urged her to "prepare more earnestly for your real calling, the only calling of a young woman—I mean the state of a housewife."

A year later Fanny married the artist Wilhelm Hensel, who produced many drawings of the Mendelssohn family. She lived her musical life through her brother's career. ◆

ANTI-SEMITISM

Of all the many examples of cruelty in human history, none is more terrible than anti-Semitism, the continuing perse-cution of the Jewish people. In the Middle Ages, ignorant and superstitious Christians believed that Jews were evil. Jews were blamed for the bubonic plague that devastated Europe in the 14th Century. People believed that Jews poisoned the village wells. Another common belief was that Jews killed Christian babies and used their blood in religious rituals. Many other stories were just as horrible.

Adolf Hitler

During the Spanish Inquisition that began late in the 15th Century, Judaism (the Jewish religion) was declared a crime. People found guilty were burned at the stake. In Poland and Lithuania, massacres of Jews were common. Towns all over Europe passed laws making life miserable for the Jewish people.

In Germany Jews could not manufacture goods. They could not own land. They could not sell food except to other Jews. They were forced to live in ghettos, crowded areas in the worst parts of the cities. They had to pay various kinds of taxes. They were forbidden to learn German. When times became hard for everyone, Jews were driven out of their homes and forced to move to other towns or other countries.

Later in the 18th Century, during a period called the Enlightenment, there was more tolerance. Laws were passed in some countries granting Jews equality with other citizens. The United States passed an equality law in 1789. France passed a similar law in 1791. Germany did not pass an equality law until 1871. But even in countries where there were equality laws, people continued to hate Jews and treat them unfairly. Some Jews converted to Christianity, but they were still considered to be alien.

Anti-Semitism in Germany increased in spite of the equality law. After he came to power in 1933, Adolf Hitler and his followers denied that Jews had ever contributed to German culture. They destroyed the works of Jewish writers, artists, and musicians.

Far worse, the Germans followed Hitler's orders and murdered millions of Jews in what is known as the Holocaust. It is one of the most horrible examples of genocide—the attempt to eliminate an entire people—the world has ever known.

This portrait of Felix Mendelssohn as a boy reveals his serious nature. Far from being spoiled by his family's wealth, Felix spent long hours studying and practicing his music. He also was an accomplished artist and writer. During his teenage years Felix traveled widely. He visited the famous German writer Goethe when he was twelve years old. They became good friends in spite of the 60 years difference in their ages.

A Happy Childhood

The name Felix means "happy." By most of the ways that we measure happiness, Felix Mendelssohn had a very fitting name. He had the full support of a close and loving family. The family was also rich, so he never had to worry about how to make a living. Still, the standards and expectations of such a family can be as great a pressure as poverty.

Abraham Mendelssohn devoted himself to his children. With his wealth, he tried to protect them from the prejudice against Jews. So in March of 1816, the children were baptized as Christians. They also added the name of one of Lea's brothers who had converted to Christianity to their own name: Mendelssohn-Bartholdy. Abraham and Lea were baptized six years later. Moses Mendelssohn would have been shocked had he lived to see where his ideas of tolerance would lead his son!

The children were too young—Felix was only seven and Fanny barely eleven—to understand what was going on. Fanny later wrote a letter to Felix in which she called Bartholdy "this name which we all dislike." The whole question of religion did not seem as important to them as the effort to lead a good and productive life.

The children began their day at 5:00 a.m. Their tutors kept them busy studying languages, science, mathematics, history, art, and, of course, music. They also developed their physical abilities with gymnastics, swimming, horseback riding, and dancing.

Besides his talent in music, Felix was very good at drawing. His landscape sketching continued throughout his life. He also wrote very well. He sent over 7,000 letters to his family, friends and teachers. These provide a great deal of information about his life.

Of all his music teachers, Zelter was the most important. He taught Felix the musical methods of Bach and other great composers. The boy developed a love of the music of the past that would continue through his career.

Zelter was a friend of the great German writer Johann Wolfgang von Goethe. When Felix was twelve years old, Zelter took him on a trip to Weimar to visit Goethe.

Felix's sister Fanny had made him promise to tell her everything about his trip. In a letter he said, "I play far more here than I do at home, seldom for less than four hours, often for six and sometimes as many as eight hours. Every afternoon Goethe opens his piano and says: 'I haven't heard you yet today, play something for me.'... You can't imagine how kind and gracious he is."

For the two weeks they were in Weimar, Felix was treated like part of Goethe's family. The twelve-year-old boy and the seventy-two-year-old poet developed a close friendship.

Felix traveled a lot during his teenage years. In 1822 the entire family went on a three-month trip to Switzerland. Felix was delighted with the magnificent landscapes of the mountains, and with yodeling. He wrote to Zelter, "Certainly this kind of singing sounds harsh and unpleasant when it is heard near-by or in a room. But it

sounds beautiful when you hear it with mingling or answering echoes, in the valleys or on the mountains or in the woods." This combining of music with natural sounds would be an important element of Felix's music.

Although he was only thirteen years old, the music he was writing was mature. The quality and the quantity of his work continued to grow. He wrote piano quartets, and sonatas for viola and clarinet. In 1824 he wrote his first symphony for full orchestra.

That year he also wrote his fourth opera, *The Uncle from Boston*. After its first performance, Zelter stood before the audience and said, "My dear boy, from this day you are no longer an apprentice, but a full member of the brotherhood of musicians. I proclaim you independent, in the name of Mozart, Haydn, and old father Bach."

Still, Felix's anxious parents were not sure that their son should be a professional musician. The following year Abraham Mendelssohn took his son on a trip to Paris. He wanted to get the opinion of Luigi Cherubini, the famous composer who was director of the Paris Conservatory.

Cherubini listened to one of Felix's piano quartets and was impressed. He said, "The boy will do well; he already does well." Felix met many other musical celebrities besides Cherubini. But he was very critical of Paris and its music. When Fanny told him that his letters contained nothing but criticism, he answered her, "Do think a little, I beg of you! Are you in Paris or am I? So I really ought to know better than you."

When Felix and his father returned from Paris, the Mendelssohn family moved to a new home. It was a magnificent estate on the outskirts of Berlin. Felix's mother described their property in a letter to her cousin: "A whole row of rooms opens on

to a garden, which is itself surrounded by other gardens, and that is why one doesn't hear any carriages or see anyone, and why there is no dust." Behind the gardens there was a large meadow, and a farm which produced fresh milk for the family.

The Mendelssohns hardly ever went away from their home, except to travel. The cultural and intellectual society of Berlin came to them. Among their regular guests were important writers, scientists, and philosophers. And of course important musicians.

Italian composer Luigi Cherubini (1760-1842) held a dominant position in European music. He was Director of the French Conservatoire in Paris. Felix Mendelssohn's father consulted with Cherubini before deciding that a career in music would be suitable for the boy.

According to one guest, the members of the Mendelssohn family "led a fantastic, dreamlike life...like one uninterrupted festival day, full of poetry, music, merry games, ingenious practical jokes, disguises and representations."

On Sundays the Mendelssohns had musical evenings. Fanny and Felix played their own compositions for their guests. In this setting, Felix composed some of his finest music. In the autumn of

This romantic picture of Felix and his sister Fanny emphasizes the close relationship between brother and sister. Fanny, however, was no passive wilting admirer. She was an active force in her brother's creative life. Many who heard both of them play, and who were familiar with their compositions, believed that Fanny's musical genius equaled or even surpassed her brother's. Their father believed that a career in music was not suitable for a woman and told Fanny to prepare for a life as a housewife.

1825, he completed an octet for four violins, two violas and two cellos. It was one of the 19th Century's greatest works of chamber music. It sustained counterpoint for all eight parts. This was an amazing achievement and showed how well Felix had learned his lessons from the masters of baroque music.

The Octet was far more than a demonstration of difficult technique. It also has the light and charming style of Mendelssohn's greatest works. Fanny described it by saying, "One feels so near the world of spirits, carried away in the air, half inclined to snatch up a broomstick and follow the aerial procession. At the end the first violin takes flight with a feather-like lightness and—all has vanished."

In 1826, the summer of his 17th year, Felix wrote his famous overture to Shakespeare's *A Midsummer Night's Dream*. Perhaps the happy summer seemed like the enchanted world of Shakespeare's play. Felix was able to capture the world of fairies and young lovers beautifully in his music.

While he was still a teenager, Felix Mendelssohn had already produced works of genius. They were works that indicated he would soon outgrow the small world of his family's luxurious home. He would also soon outgrow the limited cultural world of Berlin.◆

Goethe

One of the greatest writers in Western literature is Johann Wolfgang von Goethe. Born in 1749, Goethe became famous in 1774 with his first novel, *The Sorrows of Young Werther.* It is the story of a sensitive young man who falls in love with his friend's girlfriend. His love is hopeless and he commits suicide.

Goethe's novel influenced young writers, artists, and musicians. It expressed the Romantic ideal of the sensitive young man of deep feelings who was true to his own ideals. It became wildly popular and was soon translated into all the languages of Europe.

As a young man, Goethe lived the kind of stormy and emotional life that he wrote about. While others were influenced by his work and lived that way, Goethe himself became a responsible public servant. He moved to the small court of Weimar in central Germany where he served Duke Karl August. He managed the financial affairs of the court. He also was interested in scientific research.

In 1786 he made a long journey to Italy. The ancient ruins he saw there inspired his interest in classical art. When he returned to Weimar the Duke released Goethe from government duties so he could devote his time to his writing and to directing the court theater.

Although he didn't travel much after his trip to Italy, Goethe was closely involved in the cultural life of Europe. Famous writers, artists, musicians, philosophers, and scientists traveled to Weimar to visit him.

In 1795, he published another important novel, *Wilhelm Meister's Apprenticeship.* This time his hero, like Goethe himself, was disappointed with love. So he devoted his life to art, where he found happiness.

Goethe remained at Weimar for his entire adult life, except for a short period when he had to leave because the French attacked Prussia. For most of his life he worked on his masterpiece, *Faust,* a play about a scholar who sold his soul to the devil. It was finally completed in 1832, the same year that he died.

Felix Mendelssohn's devotion to music went far beyond his own brilliant compositions. As director of many successful music festivals throughout Europe, and as director of the famous Leipzig Gewandhaus Orchestra, he presented the finest music of the past and promoted the works of younger composers as well. Usually his concerts would include only one, or at the most two, of his own works. He was one of the most respected conductors of his time.

CHAPTER

4

Out into the World

N o earthly paradise lasts forever. That was true of the
Mendelssohn's private paradise in Berlin.

In 1827 the director of a Berlin theater agreed to stage a pro-
duction of Felix's comic opera *The Wedding of Camacho*. Quite likely
Felix's father did some persuading to have the theater produce his
son's work. But the audience did not like it. Felix ran out of the
theater before the performance was over. Reviews that soon appeared in newspapers were critical.

There were tensions in the Mendelssohn family, too. However
perfect their life seemed, it wasn't without stress. Felix's fame was
hard on his younger sister and brother. Rebecka, who was an excellent singer, wrote later: "My older brother and sister stole my repu-
tation as an artist. In any other family I would have been highly
regarded as a musician and perhaps been leader of a group. Next to
Felix and Fanny, I could not aspire to any recognition."

Felix and his brother Paul had at least one fight. In a letter
Felix wrote to Paul later, he remembered "the morning when we
were quarrelling so awfully and I threw you off the chair, whereupon you scratched me, whereupon I told on you, whereupon you
couldn't stand me, whereupon I became very angry."

The family did all work together in rehearsing and performing the *St. Matthew Passion*. On that positive note Felix set out almost immediately to seek his fortune. He was twenty years old. It was time for him to find out whether he could succeed in the world without the support and protection of his wealthy and powerful father.

With his parents' encouragement he traveled for nearly three years. His goal was to find the best city in which he could pursue his musical career.

London, where he arrived after four stormy, seasick days, was the first stop.

He had several reasons for starting his tour there. One was that he had good friends in the city. Another was that the director of the London Philharmonic Society, Sir George Smart, had visited the Mendelssohn home in Berlin and urged Felix to visit London. Felix had studied English and spoke it well, so language wasn't a problem. Quite likely he was also aware that England was the most tolerant of the European countries. Anti-Semitism was not as big a problem in London as it was in Berlin and other cities.

After he had been in London for more than a month, a concert was arranged in which he conducted his First Symphony. He wrote home: "The success was greater than I could ever have dreamt...At the end they applauded me as long as I kept thanking the orchestra, and shook hands till I left the hall."

A few days later Felix gave a piano recital. He wrote, "By God, I play better here than in Berlin, and that's because the people listen better. Don't take that as conceit, but it is thrilling when you feel you succeed and give others pleasure."

His greatest success came at a charity concert he organized. Felix asked some of the best opera singers in London to perform. His friend Ignaz Moscheles joined him playing his two-piano concerto. He conducted his *A Midsummer Night's Dream* Overture. As he had with his performance of Bach in Berlin, Felix proved that he was a very capable concert organizer. London and Mendelssohn began the mutual admiration that would continue throughout his career. Though he did not choose London as the city he would settle in, he visited England nearly every year.

After the musical season on his first visit, Felix and his friend Carl Klingemann went on a walking tour of Scotland. They were impressed with the rugged landscapes and wild storms. Felix made many beautiful sketches. He began his "Scottish" Symphony while visiting the palace where Queen Mary had lived. But the symphony would have to wait for 12 years before it would be completed. The same trip also gave him the inspiration for *The Hebrides*, a concert overture that is a classic of music about the sea.

By the end of the summer, Felix planned to return to Berlin for Fanny's wedding. But he was thrown from a carriage and badly hurt his knee. So he had to stay in bed for several weeks and missed the ceremony. He didn't arrive home until December, in time for his parents' silver wedding celebration. The holidays were warm and happy for the family and their friends. After that, however, Berlin disappointed Felix again.

He wrote his "Reformation" Symphony for the 300th anniversary of Martin Luther's Augsberg Confession in 1830. However, he was not invited to participate in this celebration of the Lutheran faith. The symphony wasn't premiered for two more years and by then Mendelssohn had lost confidence in it. It wasn't published until after his death. For that reason, it is officially his Fifth Symphony even though it was actually the second one he composed.

After this disappointment, Felix left Berlin again. He visited his friend Goethe in Weimar, and then went on to Munich, Salzburg, and Vienna. By autumn he was in Italy. After traveling to Venice, Bologna, and Florence, he spent the winter in Rome. Like most northern visitors, he was delighted with the climate and with the art—with the exception of Italian music, which he thought was awful.

He spent the following winter in Paris, which he enjoyed more than he had on his first visit when he was fifteen years old. Then in April, 1832, he went on to England, where he wrote, "How glad I am to be here, how dear everything seems, how I rejoice in the friendship of old acquaintances." Once more his work was praised.

In May he learned that Zelter, his friend and teacher, had died. This left the position of director of the Berlin Singakademie vacant. Felix headed home. His travels had made him certain of where he belonged. As he wrote to his father: "First, let me review what you defined as the purpose of my journey. I was to observe closely various countries and select the one in which I plan to live and work. Further, I was to make my name and capabilities known so that those I finally decided to settle among would receive me and not be wholly ignorant of my capacity. I am happy to say that I believe I have done this. The country is Germany. I am now absolutely certain."

But where in Germany? Berlin, the city where he had grown up? But Berlin would once again disappoint him.

PRUSSIA

The political and economic conditions of Germany during the 18th and 19th Centuries were confusing. It was rather like what the United States might be like if there were no central government in Washington, D.C. The many German princes each had their own little state. Sometimes they were at war with each other, and sometimes they joined together to fight against other countries. Many of the wars were about religion.

Otto von Bismark

In the north and central part of modern-day Germany, most of the people were Protestants. In the south and west they were Catholic. There was no real freedom of religion because people had to follow the beliefs of the prince who controlled the area they lived in. After a long civil war—called the Thirty Years War because it was between 1618 and 1648—the Prussian state became a major power in the affairs of Europe.

Several strong rulers helped Prussia to develop. Frederick II, who was known as Frederick the Great, ruled from 1740 to 1786. He personally controlled all aspects of his government. He had no respect for his officials. He once said, "I could hang 99 percent of them with a clear conscience." Frederick formed the attitudes of Prussia. Prussians were methodical, hard-working, and had a strong sense of duty and public service. The result was a government that was honest and productive. But it also prevented initiative and personal inquiry. Anyone who displeased Frederick could be put into prison.

The capital of Prussia was Berlin, which became one of the most conservative cities in Germany. Frederick was an unbeliever. Neither Protestant nor Catholic, he didn't think God created the monarchy. Because of this he was considered part of the Enlightenment, which promoted religious tolerance. Probably, however, Frederick was just not interested in religion. He was much more interested in the military development of Prussia. The Prussian army became a model of efficiency and discipline.

Under the leadership of Prussian chancellor Otto von Bismarck, Germany became unified in 1871. Berlin was the capital and the ideals developed in Prussia became central to the new nation. The powerful German armies embarked on two world wars during the first half of the 20th Century.

Felix Mendelssohn frequently played for Queen Victoria and Prince Albert when he toured England. Mendelssohn was greatly admired in England, which he visited nearly every year. He first met the young Queen Victoria in 1842 when she had been monarch for only five years. Victoria and her adored husband Albert loved music and loved to sing duets. When in London, Felix was invited to Buckingham Palace where he would play and the queen and prince would sing.

CHAPTER

5

Music Maker

Two candidates were being considered to replace Zelter: his assistant Carl Rungenhagen and Felix Mendelssohn. Felix appeared to be in a strong position. The Singakademie's greatest triumph had been Felix's performance of the *St. Matthew Passion*. The Mendelssohn family was among the most generous supporters of the Singakademie.

But that support worked against Felix. Many people said that the Mendelssohns were trying to buy the director's position. And even though his family had converted to Christianity, in many people's eyes they were still Jews.

So when the voting took place in 1833, Felix lost.

The Mendelssohns were angry. They withdrew all support, cutting themselves off from the musical scene in Berlin. Although it was a bitter defeat, Felix had prospects elsewhere. The Philharmonic Society invited him back to London. Felix was also invited to Düsseldorf to conduct the Lower Rhine Music Festival. He left Berlin in April.

Once away from the Prussian capital, Felix again experienced triumph after triumph. His Scottish Symphony was a sensation in

London. The music festival in Düsseldorf was such an outstanding success that he was offered the position of the town's music director. He accepted.

In a letter to a friend, Felix admitted that while his duties were to direct the church music and the Vocal Association, and perhaps a new theater that was being built, his real purpose was to have "quiet and leisure for composition. The country and the people suit me admirably."

The position in Düsseldorf was an important step in his professional career. His father, who was at the music festival, wrote home about "the useful and important school it will be for him."

It was a useful school, although not always a pleasant one. Felix had always been very critical. He found the instrumental musicians in Düsseldorf incompetent. Düsseldorf was a Catholic city, and he did not approve of the church music. He wrote to his sister Rebecka that nowhere could he find "even one tolerable mass, and not a single one of the old Italian masters; nothing but modern showiness."

He had to travel to other Catholic cities to find music to work with. When the theater opened, Mendelssohn was also responsible for producing operas. There were so many distractions that he found very little time for his own compositions.

"When I sat down to my work in the morning, at every bar there was a ringing at the bell," he wrote, "then came grumbling choristers to be snubbed, stupid singers to be taught, seedy musicians to be engaged; and when this had gone on the whole day, and I felt that these things were for the sole benefit and advantage of the Düsseldorf theatre, I was provoked."

The basic problem was that Felix was a perfectionist, and he was unable to get perfection from the musicians he had to work with. A little over a year after arriving in Düsseldorf, he resigned his post at the theater. He gradually withdrew from his other commitments as well.

But he soon got an offer from the city of Leipzig to direct their Gewandhaus Orchestra. The offer also included six months of vacation to work on his own compositions.

When he arrived in Leipzig in 1835, he found a bustling city that was the center of the music publishing business. He also found that the Gewandhaus Orchestra was composed of good musicians. One of Felix's first efforts was to raise the salaries of the musicians. They responded by giving him their full support.

But as his professional life was beginning to thrive, his personal life suffered a tragedy.

In November of 1835 Abraham Mendelssohn died suddenly. Felix wrote to his friend Klingemann, "In what manner my life can go on I've no idea, not as yet."

His life did go on with the dedication to service and hard work that his father had taught him. The Gewandhaus concerts became so popular that people started to complain that they needed a larger hall. Felix presented the people of Leipzig with a large variety of music. He arranged all-Beethoven concerts, Mozart concerts, and a series of historical concerts that featured a range of old masters.

He was equally energetic in presenting the best music of his contemporaries such as Robert Schumann, a younger composer who lived and worked in Leipzig. He never pushed his own music.

Throughout his career Mendelssohn considered it his duty to present the greatest music, whatever the age that had produced it.

"If you really feel for what is beautiful, if it truly gladdens you, then your mind becomes enlarged rather than narrowed," he wrote to his sister Rebecka. "I always get upset when some praise only Beethoven, others only Palestrina and still others only Mozart or Bach. All four of them I say, or none at all."

Soon Felix Mendelssohn was one of the best-known conductors in Germany. In 1836 he went to Frankfurt to conduct. There he met nineteen-year-old Cécile Jeanrenaud, and fell in love. They were married the following March.

Marriage did not slow down Felix's busy work schedule. After a brief honeymoon he was off to England to conduct the Birmingham Festival and perform in London. Then it was back to Leipzig where he arrived after lunch on the day he was to conduct the first concert of the season. In spite of the hectic pace of Felix's career, his marriage was a happy and peaceful one because of Cécile's gentle and understanding nature. They had four children.

In 1841 Felix and his family moved reluctantly to Berlin. The new ruler of Prussia, Wilhelm IV, had decreed that Berlin was to be the capital of German culture, with an Academy of Arts that included architecture, music, painting, and sculpture. Felix was invited to be composer for the Royal Theatre, director of the Royal Orchestra, and conductor and organizer of the Cathedral choir. It was, of course, a great honor. And being close to his family appealed to him. Furthermore, his salary would be three times what he was paid in Leipzig. So, in spite of his misgivings about Berlin, Felix accepted the king's offer. He still maintained his post in Leipzig. And he accepted guest conducting performances all over Europe.

In modern terms, we might call Felix Mendelssohn a workaholic. His health began to suffer.

What happened in Berlin didn't help. The king proved to be the sort who had good ideas but did not carry them out. The funds for the Arts Academy were never adequate. The musicians Felix had to work with were second-rate. He endured the frustrations for three years before abandoning the position and going back to Leipzig.

His adopted city welcomed him back joyously. Felix set to work on a project he had wanted for a long time, a music conservatory. He brought together an excellent faculty, and he taught piano and composition classes himself. He noted that the most talented students were frequently too poor to pay for lessons, so he established scholarships. But for all his continued success in Leipzig, it was England that admired Mendelssohn the most.

Felix met the young Queen Victoria in 1842. She had been Queen for only five years. She and her husband, Prince Albert, both enjoyed music and loved to sing duets. When Felix was in London he was invited to Buckingham Palace where he would play and Victoria and Albert would sing.

The following year he wrote what is his most frequently played composition. The "Wedding March" is the joyous conclusion to hundreds of thousands of marriage ceremonies every year. The happy bride and groom walk arm-in-arm up the aisle to the strains of Felix's music in their first moments as a married couple.

Felix prepared his oratorio *Elijah* for the Birmingham Festival of 1846. He was asked to return the following year to conduct the oratorio in London. Once again he couldn't say no. And the one performance turned into six, four in London and one each in

Manchester and Birmingham. The day before the Birmingham concert Felix conducted his Scottish Symphony and *A Midsummer Night's Dream* Overture at the Philharmonic Society, and was soloist in a Beethoven Piano Concerto. He also made a number of chamber performances and made two appearances at Buckingham Palace in addition to giving receptions for the Prussian Ambassador. By the time he started for home, he was so exhausted he could barely walk.

Felix had only been home for a few days when he received the greatest blow of his life. Fanny had died of a stroke. Felix collapsed when he heard of her death. He wrote, "She was part of me every moment of my life. There was no joy I experienced without thinking of the joy she would feel with me...I have not been able to think about music; when I try to do so, everything in me seems desolate and empty."

Cécile took him on a trip to Switzerland, where he did some drawings and water colors but had difficulty working at his music. He went for long walks alone. When they returned to Leipzig, he could not return to his duties. He had a series of strokes during the second half of October. On the fourth of November, 1847 he died. He was only 38 years old. ◆

Queen Victoria

Queen Victoria ruled England longer than any other king or queen. Her reign lasted for 64 years, from 1837 to 1901. Her father was Edward, Duke of Kent, who married a German princess. Victoria, their only child, was born in 1819. Edward died when the baby was only eight months old.

Edward's brothers were two English kings, George IV and William IV. But neither had any children to succeed him as heir to the throne. That meant that Victoria would become queen when William died.

If King William died before Victoria was 18 years old, then her ambitious mother would become regent and have control of the country. But the King hated Victoria's mother. He managed to stay alive for 27 days after Victoria's 18th birthday, and therefore the young girl became queen.

As it turned out, Victoria didn't like her mother very much either. As soon as she became Queen of England, Victoria refused to be influenced by her mother. Since she was only eighteen, and had been raised almost entirely in isolation, she did need guidance. She respected Lord Melbourne, the Prime Minister. He became almost like a father to Victoria and they worked well together.

In 1839 Victoria's German-born cousin Albert came to England for a visit. The young queen fell in love with him. They were married the following year and Albert became the strongest influence in her life. Victoria adored him and followed his advice about nearly everything she did. They produced nine children, four sons and five daughters, who married members of other European royal families. Since she and Albert kept close control of their children, Queen Victoria's influence was felt throughout Europe. When Albert died in 1861, she was devastated. She wore black mourning clothing for the rest of her life.

Victoria's long reign was conservative politically and reflected the values of the middle class in art and morality. The term "Victorian" has come to mean prudish and repressed when it is applied to behavior and artistic expression.

Selected Works

Orchestral Music
Symphony No. 3, the "Scotch"
Symphony No. 4, the "Italian"
Symphony No. 5, the "Reformation"
Overtures to *Midsummer Night's Dream,*
    Ruy Blas, and *Hebrides*
Concerto for violin and orchestra
Concerto for piano and orchestra No. 1
Concerto for piano and orchestra No. 2

Piano Music
48 Songs Without Words, among them
    "Spring Song," "Venetian Boat
    Songs," "Hunting Song," "Spinning
    Song," and the "Funeral March"

Chamber Music
Octet for strings
Quartet No. 1
Quartet No. 6

Choral Music
Elijah oratorio
St. Paul oratorio

Chronology

1809 born in Hamburg, Germany on February 3
1811 family flees from Hamburg to Berlin
1815 begins piano lessons
1816 visits Paris
1817 begins studying music with Carl Zelter
1818 first public appearance as pianist
1821 visits Johann Wolfgang von Goethe at Weimar
1825 visits Paris and is examined by Luigi Cherubini
1826 composes Overture to *A Midsummer Night's Dream*
1829 conducts revival of Bach's *St. Matthew Passion*; first visit to England
1831 travels to Italy
1833 rejected as director of Berlin Singakademie after Zelter's death
1835 appointed director of Leipzig Gewandhaus; father dies
1837 marries Cécile Jeanrenaud; travels to England
1842 "Scottish" Symphony finished and played in Leipzig and London; meets Queen Victoria; mother dies
1843 opening of Leipzig Conservatory
1846 first performance of *Elijah* at Birmingham Festival; returns to Leipzig ill
1847 sister Fanny dies of a stroke on May 14; soon becomes very ill and dies in Leipzig on November 4

Timeline in History

1809 composer Joseph Haydn dies; Napoleon battles Austria and occupies Vienna

1812 United States declares war on Britain; Napoleon attacks Russia

1815 Wellington defeats Napoleon at Waterloo

1820 Sir Walter Scott writes *Ivanhoe*; King George III of England dies

1824 King Louis XVIII of France dies; composer Ludwig van Beethoven writes his Ninth Symphony

1827 Beethoven dies; Turks capture Acropolis in Athens

1831 Charles Darwin sails on the *Beagle*

1834 slavery abolished in the British Empire

1837 Victoria becomes Queen of England

1840 Frederick William III of Prussia dies, succeeded by Frederick William IV

1844 Alexander Dumas publishes *The Three Musketeers* and *The Count of Monte Cristo*

1847 Emily Bronte publishes *Wuthering Heights*; Charlotte Bronte publishes *Jane Eyre*

1848 gold is discovered in California

For Further Reading

For Young Readers

Hurd, Michael. *Mendelssohn*. New York: Thomas Y. Crowell Company, 1970.
Kamen, Gloria. *Hidden Music: The Life of Fanny Mendelssohn*. New York: Atheneum Books for Young Readers, 1996.

Works Consulted:

Blunt, Wilfrid. *On Wings of Song: a Biography of Felix Mendelssohn*. New York: Charles Scribner's Sons, 1974.
Elvers, Rudolf (ed.). *Felix Mendelssohn: A Life in Letters*. Trans. Craig Tomlinson. New York: Fromm International Publishing Corp., 1986.
Jacob, Heinrich Eduard. *Felix Mendelssohn and His Times*. Trans. Richard and Clara Winston. Englewood Cliffs, NJ: Prentice-Hall Inc., 1963.
Jenkins, David and Mark Visocchi. *Mendelssohn in Scotland*. London: Chappell & Company Ltd., 1978.
Kaufman, Schima. *Mendelssohn: A Second Elijah*. New York: Tudor Publishing Co., 1936.
Kupferberg, Herbert. *The Mendelssohns: Three Generations of Genius*. New York: Charles Scribner's Sons, 1972.
Marek, George R. *Gentle Genius: The Story of Felix Mendelssohn*. New York: Funk & Wagnalls, 1972.
Mercer-Taylor, Peter. *The Life of Mendelssohn*. Cambridge, UK: Cambridge University Press, 2000
Moshansky, Mozelle. *Mendelssohn, His Life and Times*. New York: Hippocrene Books, 1982.
Radcliffe, Philip. *Mendelssohn*. Oxford, UK: Oxford University Press, 2000.

On the Internet:

Classical Music Pages: Felix Mendelssohn (-Bartholdy) (1809-1847)
http://www.rz-berlin.mpg.de/comp.lst/Mendelssohn.html

Classical Net: Felix Mendelssohn
http://www.classicalnet/music/comp.lst/mendelssohn.html

Felix Mendelssohn Biography
http://www.geocities.com/Paris/3486.mend.html

Felix Mendelssohn: Biographical Notes
http://www.gaglianorecordings.com/mendbio.html

Glossary

baroque (buh-ROKE) - highly decorated form of art that flourished in the 17th and 18th Centuries

blockade (blah-KADE) - attempt to starve an enemy by preventing goods from reaching him

chamber music (CHAYM-bur MEW-zik) - music written for a small number of performers

counterpoint (KOWN-ter-poynt) - art of combining two or more melodies simultaneously

ghetto (GET-toe) - portion of a city in which Jews or other minorities are forced to reside

octet (ock-TET) - piece of chamber music written for eight musicians

oratorio (or-uh-TORE-ee-oh) - dramatic musical composition, usually on a religious theme

overture (OH-ver-chur) - orchestral piece to be performed before the raising of the curtain in an opera or other theater presentation

passion (PASH-un) - musical work based on the suffering and crucifixion of Jesus Christ

quartet (kwor-TET) - piece of chamber music written for four musicians

score (SKOHR) - copy of a piece of music showing all the parts

symphony (SIM-fun-ee) - extended musical composition in sonata form for full orchestra

Index

Bach, Johann Sebastian 7, 8, 10, 13, 24, 25, 40

Baroque music 6, 13

Beethoven, Ludwig 10, 40, 45

Berlin Singakademie 9, 34, 37, 44

Cherubini, Luigi 25, 26, 44

Devrient, Eduard 9, 10, 19

Devrient, Therese 8, 9

Goethe, Johann 24, 29, 34, 44

Handel, George Frideric 13

Haydn, Joseph 10, 25, 45

Hensel, Wilhelm 20

Klingemann, Carl 33, 39

Ledbetter, Stephen 10

Mendelssohn, Felix

    brother, Paul Mendelssohn 18, 31

    education 19

    father, Abraham Mendelssohn 17, 18, 19, 23, 25, 38, 39, 44

    grandfather, Moses Mendelssohn 15,16,17

grandmother, Babette Salomon 8

grandmother, Fromet Guggenheim Mendelssohn 16

mother, Lea Salomon Mendelssohn 17, 18, 23, 25, 44

musical compositions 25, 26, 28, 30, 31, 33, 41, 44

sister, Rebekah 8, 18, 31, 38

sister, Fanny 8, 18, 19, 23, 24, 25, 26, 27, 28, 33, 42, 44

wife, Cecile Jeanrenaud Mendelssohn 40, 42, 44

Moscheles, Ignaz 33

Mozart, Wolfgang Amadeus 7, 10, 25, 40

Napoleon 14, 17, 18, 45

Queen Victoria 36, 41, 43, 45

Schumann, Robert 39

Zelter, Carl 7, 8, 9, 24, 25, 34, 37, 44